I dedicate this book to my daughter, Coa.
I hope your drawing talents fly higher than
Freedom's flights.

www.mascotbooks.com

Freedom's Highest Flight

For more information, please contact:
Mascot Books
620 Herndon Parkway, Suite 320
Herndon, VA 20170
info@mascotbooks.com

Library of Congress Control Number:2018909156

CPSIA Code: PRTWP1218A
ISBN-13: 978-1-64307-166-4

Printed in Malaysia

FREEDOM'S HIGHEST FLIGHT

Casey McCall Corbett

Illustrated by Patrick Powell

It was a windy day for Freedom to fly.

And the strong wind soon took him way too high.

He knew he needed to get down to the field and fast,

But flying against this wind was just too much of a task.

He saw the soccer field and started going that way,

When he heard a loud voice yell, "Wait! Don't fly away.

Many tales about you I've heard.

It's a great honor to meet such a majestic bird."

"You've got a job to do and you must fly down.

You represent so much to the people of this town.

You see, you and I are very much the same.

Let me explain why you're so important to this game.

"My name is Erskine Russell, but everyone called me Erk.

In 1981 I was asked to bring back football, which many said wouldn't work.

Money was tight, and we had no field on which to play.

I transported my players on two old yellow school buses each day.

"My first football players were just homegrown men

Who wanted to play football, and more importantly, had the heart to win.

These guys were tough and they loved the game.

Nothing would stop them, not even a category 4 hurricane.

"There's a ditch near the practice field we crossed over many times each week.

I named this trickling water Beautiful Eagle Creek.

That magical liquid had powers only I could see.

And sprinkling it on opposing fields brought us many victories.

"The option offense is what I coached my men to play.

It was so effective, it's still used to this day.

The double option, the triple option—there are so many plays to run.

Instead of under the center, my quarterback sometimes went from the shotgun.

"To the fullback he might've handed the ball quick

Or pitched it to either halfback before he took a hit.

He could keep it himself and run it real hard.

It was always exciting watching that QB roll up those yards.

"One option team I hold dear to my heart

Was led by a quarterback no one was willing to start.

I took a chance on his passing skills and speed,

Because I knew he's what the new team did need.

The Hambone offense put lots of points on the board.

Averaging 41.3 a game was something no one could ignore.

"It was in 1985 we won our first National Championship game.

And in 1986 we did the same.

It was my last year in 1989 when we had our third win.

Then in 1990, Coach Tim Stowers won a national championship yet again.

In 1999 and 2000 Coach Paul Johnson added two more,

But that wasn't the end—Eagle football had more in store.

"The football world was stunned when we traveled to the swamp.

It was in Gainesville, Florida, where we put a stop to the gator chomp.

Who says you can't run the option and win?

Those Eagles ran 429 yards, my friend.

We ran the triple option with such class,

Beating those Gators 26-20 without ever completing a pass.

"Winning a Southern Conference Championship ten times is great.

But when the Eagles moved up to the Sun Belt, they just couldn't wait.

They surprised a lot of people that first year in

As they brought home a Sun Belt Conference Championship win.

"In Mobile, Alabama, you were there with the team

When they took on and beat Bowling Green.

The GoDaddy Bowl was a historical first.

It started off close but ended with a scoring burst.

Those Eagles made me so very proud!

Along with everyone else wearing blue and white in that crowd.

"So you see, my young bird,

There's a legacy that has to be heard.

You must fly down to the gridiron below.

Get to the field and let everyone know.

"As solid as the oak trees on Sweetheart Circle stand,

Eagle nation has the strongest bond known to man.

We have the greatest team in America through and through.

It's a love, loyalty, and allegiance that is always True Blue.

"On mighty wings you soar my friend.

You've done this time and time again.

Fly into Paulson Stadium to that Eagle goal line,

And help my boys win 'just one more time.'"

Freedom

Freedom was just a tiny, white ball of fuzz when he was found knocked out of his nest in Maitland, Florida, in 2004. He was taken to the Florida Audubon Center for Birds of Prey, where he was examined for any injuries. It was their initial hope he would be treated and then released back into the wild to live the ordinary life of a bald eagle. Sadly, that was not the case. He had an infection and an injury to his beak. It was not clear if the beak injury was sustained in the fall or if it was a birth defect. Regardless, with a misaligned beak it was apparent he would not have survived long in the wild and it is the reason he would never return to an ordinary life of a bald eagle. But fate stepped in; this young eaglet was not meant to live an ordinary life.

That same year the U. S. Fish and Wildlife Service decided to place this young eagle at the Center for Wildlife Education and Lamar Q Ball, Jr. Raptor Center at Georgia Southern University. This majestic bird, the symbol of our country and the University, was given the name Freedom. And it is due to the Wildlife Center he is able to live the extraordinary life he was meant to live. Whether he flies around Paulson Stadium during his home pregame flights or over the heads of the graduating seniors of the University, he is an ambassador to all wildlife on the ground and in the air. He represents not only Georgia Southern University, but our great nation and is an excellent reminder of our honorable military who make sacrifices so we can all remain free.

Wildlife Center

The origin of the Center for Wildlife Education and Lamar Q Ball, Jr. Raptor Center began from a nationally televised mistake in 1990. On December 15th, during the Division I-AA National Championship game, a sports announcer on CBS erroneously called a large bird flying overhead a bald eagle, when it was apparent Georgia Southern was about to win their fourth national championship. The bird, unfortunately, was a turkey vulture, and is commonly called a buzzard in South Georgia. That innocent mistake did not sit well with many alumni and fans, and rather quickly led to the discussion to try to find a live bald eagle mascot.

That desire led to a phone call to Steve Hein, a master falconer from Bulloch County. He contacted the U. S. Fish and Wildlife Service and it wasn't long before a rehabilitated, but flightless, five-year-old female bald eagle was placed at Georgia Southern University. She was given the name Glory.

Little did anyone realize it was not just her destiny to become Georgia Southern University's first live mascot, but also to be the reason to build one of the only wildlife centers on a university campus open to the public. Thanks to the misidentification of a true bald eagle and a very generous private donation, the Center for Wildlife Education and Lamar Q Ball, Jr. Raptor Center opened its doors in 1997.

Today, visitors can see Glory as she sits atop her nest on the Raptor Walkway, along with other rehabilitated birds of prey and wildlife that are incapable of being released back into the wild. At the wildlife center on campus at Georgia Southern University, these wild animals are able to continue their lives as representatives for all wildlife and are able to educate visitors about their existence and the environment, as well as the current and future impact of man and nature.